CW00665582

Con

Introduction	1
The Wonders of the Miniverse	31
Zany Views	47
Miss Cellany	65
El Paradiso	91
Lieder Here	113
Risqué Business	139
Index of first lines	158

Introduction

The following poems are intended solely as an attempt at humour. Nothing more than that.

Hopefully they are accessible to all age groups and may even lead certain readers to want to create their own comic verse. They are not written by someone with a degree or intended for analysis by those who have – a humourous poem or rhyme can improve your day and if that is achieved by any verse within these pages then that is all that matters.

The idea that words can add to the enjoyment of life has been very important to me from my early childhood in the 1950s and early 1960s in Newcastle under Lyme. Programmes on radio were a particular source of enjoyment especially the song 'Goodness Gracious Me' by Peter Sellers and Sophia Loren was one of my favourites as well as 'The Ying Tong Song' by the Goons.

My mother was a big Spike Milligan fan and she even quoted Shakespeare to me – I distinctly remember, after I had been caught being economical with the truth, her saying forcefully,

'This above all: to thine own self be true'.

My father would sometimes bring home jokes or verse that were going round his office like these:

Daredaygo fortylorisinaro
Demarntloris demartrux
Fullacowsan ensandux
(Explanation on page 157)

And the Lord said unto Moses,
All people shall have round noses,
Except Aaron,
And he shall have a square- un.

Other poems that I was introduced to, at this time, included 'The Daffodils' by William Wordsworth and 'Leisure' by W. H. Davies both of which I have included my own version in this collection.

On the TV was the programme 'Crackerjack' which often ended with a sketch including a song from the charts sung to alternative words. I will never forget my amazement when they sang a version of 'Bohemian Rhapsody'.

Later on, as a teenager I was involved in productions of Gilbert and Sullivan operas, where I came across the patter song.

I am the very model of a modern Major-General,
I've information vegetable, animal, and mineral,
I know the kings of England,
and I quote the fights historical
From Marathon to Waterloo, in order categorical;
I'm very well acquainted, too,
with matters mathematical,
I understand equations,
both the simple and quadratical,
About binomial theorem
I'm teeming with a lot o' news,

With many cheerful facts about
the square of the hypotenuse.
I'm very good at integral and differential calculus;
I know the scientific names of beings animalculous:
In short, in matters vegetable, animal, and mineral,
I am the very model of a modern Major-General.

Our home didn't have many books. I remember my father going to the saleroom ie. Visiting a local auction and bringing home four encyclopaedias called 'The World of the Children' (out of date by twenty years) and a large dictionary in two volumes. These were totally uninspiring except for some origami in 'The World of the Children'.

However we did have a copy of 'Verse and Worse' which was a poetry collection by Arnold Silcock that had been given to my mother as a wedding present. The collection had several poems that appealed to me as a child some of which I've included on the following pages.

I vividly remember reading 'Castaway' and through the clever wording being 'led up the garden path'. This poem more than any other was my initial inspiration for writing poetry. Here is the complete poem.

Castaway

He grabbed me round my slender neck,
I could not shout or scream,
He carried me into his room
Where we could not be seen;
He tore away my flimsy wrap
And gazed upon my form-
I was so cold and still and damp,
While he was wet and warm.
His feverish mouth he pressed to mine –
I let him have his way-
He drained me of my very self,
I could not say him nay.
He made me what I am. Alas!
That's why you find me here…
A broken vessel, broken glass,
That once held Bottled Beer.

Anon.

My other favourite poems from this collection are;

Manners

I eat my peas with honey;
I've done it all my life.
It makes the peas taste funny,
But it keeps 'em on the knife.

Anon

Ware Tomato-Juice

An accident happened to my brother Jim
When somebody threw a tomato at him –
Tomatoes are juicy and don't hurt the skin,
But this one was specially packed in a tin.

Anon

Manners

There was a young lady of Tottenham,
Who had no manners,
or else she'd forgotten 'em;
At tea at the vicars
She whipped off her knickers
Because, she explained, she felt 'ot in 'em.

Anon

The Rash Lady of Ryde

There was an old lady of Ryde
Who ate some green apples, and died.
The apples, (fermented inside the lamented)
And made cider inside her inside.

Anon

The Irish Pig

'Twas an evening in November,
As I very well remember,
I was strolling down the street in drunken pride,
But my knees were all a'flutter
So I landed in the gutter,
And a pig came up and lay down by my side.

Yes, I lay there in the gutter
Thinking thoughts I could not utter,
When a colleen passing by did softly say,
'Ye can tell a man who boozes
By the company he chooses' –
At that, the pig got up and walked away!

Anon

I cannot recommend 'Verse and Worse' too highly, there many hidden gems within its pages, including many longer poems.

Youjuice

'Twas an evening in September
As I very well remember,
I was walking in the jungle with my guide.
When a shriek yelled by some nutter
Made my heart go all a flutter,
And a cannibal appeared, right by my side.

Yes. I stood there (I'll not stutter)
Thinking thoughts of m..m..me with butter
When my wife with pointing gun did loudly say,
'You can tell that this defuses
When a club is all he uses'
At that the cannibal just walked away.

Limbless

She stood on the bridge at midnight
Her lips were all a quiver,
She gave a cough – her leg fell off
And floated down the river.

I wish I had written this – *(Please note that an attempt was made to find the copyright holder. If the Estate would care to contact me I would be grateful.)*

Petalpower

An accident happened
to my sister Dot
When down came a daffodil
from a high spot –
Now flowers are harmless
but this one was not,
It came sweetly scented
and wrapped in a pot.

I spent 34 years as a primary school music teacher. Always on the look-out for humorous songs to amuse the children I found that some songs benefited by being brought up to date which I enjoyed having a go at. This one went down particularly well.

Zanydood

Yankee Doodle went to town
Riding on a pony;
He stuck a feather in his hat,
And called it macaroni.

Chorus: Yankee Doodle keep it up,
Yankee Doodle dandy,
Mind the music and the step
And with the girls be handy.

Yankee Doodle had a farm,
Where he kept cows for butter,
And hens to lay him hard boiled eggs
For breakfast lunch or supper.

Yankee Doodle has a horse
It's lame of course and lazy,
And it just sits and eats and eats
And this drives Doodle crazy.

Yankee Doodle likes his beer
He drinks it by the flagon.
And you could say he needs it as
His wife she is a dragon.

Yankee Doodle often tries
To find a place that's calmer.
And you may see him on the roof
While eating a banana.

Yankee Doodle stays out late
On ev'nings when it's balmy.
And now his fav'rite takeaway,
is chicken biriami.

Yankee Doodle has false teeth,
And while his wife is cooking,
He'll creep in to the kitchen's heat
And hide them in the pudding.

Yankee Doodle visits the zoo
He likes the lions and llamas.
But they came round and threw him out
For wearing his pyjamas.

Henrietta, the pet chicken is three years old.

Chickeneggday

Happy worm day to you,
Happy squirm day to you,
Happy third birthday Henrietta,
Happy bird day to you.

Sitansetanseeon

I think that I will never get
Permission for a blue whale pet.

But if I did it'd make folks gawk
When I took it for an evening walk.

I'd like to see its massive lips
And I would feed it fish and ships.

It's monstrous tail would rise and splat
And put an end to next door's cat.

And me I'd have a plan as such
And build the most enormous hutch.

'**A BLUE WHALE**! **NO WAY**!' my mum shrieked
'I think your brain's gone up the creek!'

'You never looked after that elephant we got you!'
'But muuuuum tisn't fair!'

Just wait! (She'll reget what she said,)
I'll put a huge scorpion ....in her bed.

.....and he's my little Nipper.

Duocaped

Chorus:

Jingle bells, Batman yells,
Robin's wants a fight,
Oh! What fun it is to ride
With the Bat-duo tonight,
Jingle bells, Robin yells,
Batman's on his way.
Oh! What fun it is to ride
In the Bat-mobile today.

Flashing through the glow,
Of a city's crowded ways,
Riddler he will go,
Laughing all the way.
Mischief he will bring,
He is bound to fight,
Oh what fun it is to sing,
We'll make things right tonight.

Chorus:

Soon we both will know,
Whether it will be our day,
We are sure to go,
Laughing all the way.
Penguin's going to sing,
Jester's going to fight,
Oh what fun it is to think,
We'll bash them all tonight.

There was a young lady from Leeds,
Who swallowed a packet of seeds.
It soon came to pass
She was covered in grass
And her ears were sprouting with weeds.

Anon

Comedy captions.
Using the poem below each picture,
can you think of a suitable caption or
if there's a speech bubble, complete the text?
My answers are on page *157* but yours may be better.

1.

A Selection of portraits of Birdwatchers

A Delboy twitcher Albert Ross
Who views the birds at Charring Cross,
And earns his cash by selling meat
He's come by slyly on the street.
A business that he's always ran,
And traded from a reliant van,
The thing that in the local bar
Was referred to as his 'butchery car.

A cleric twitcher Rev. Kitti Wake
Was often seen out by the lake,
With her binoculars in hand
Taking in this verdant land.
She looks and scans the old church tower
Seeking for an avian bower,
She sees upon a narrow ledge
A juvenile about to fledge.
The parent lean windswept, blown
Sits by the crucifix of stone.
The birds are svelte. The church is grey.
They are of course all birds of pray.

The aged twitcher Colonel Pheasant
Doesn't help, he isn't pleasant,
So he berates the local youth
With what he thinks is gospel truth.
'Get your hair cut,' raises a titter.
'Don't snipe,' retorts the local vicar.
The youths' reply

'Bet he keeps his teeth in a night jar,'
'And if we harass him
He'll have one of his little turns.'
The Colonel, hearing this, isn't chuffed,
Doesn't rail as he's verbally cuffed
He simply says ' Owl see about that!'
And keeps his hair on. Doesn't grouse.
Just carries on, to see what follows,
But naught is said, his tongue he swallows.

The sixty's twitcher Randy Coot,
Who cranes his neck – the grand old fruit,
He'll hang about and always try,
To goose the girls as they pass by.
He swans around ducking and diving
(His battered sports car isn't thriving,)
He isn't swift at making lobby
And hasn't got another hobby.

Well there's a clutch of eccentric twitchers
Donning p'lovers unlike strippers,
And if grebious bodily harm is nigh,
Just throstle back and give a sigh,
Don't rail at their perplexing hobby,
Just think of Enid Blyton's Noddy.

Teacher: What do you call a sick bird of prey?
Pupil: Illegal Sir.

Horsing Around

Crossing merry England's state,
A bishop who was ready,
To stop the coach and alleviate
His need to spend a penny.

A lonely farmhouse came in view
They stopped and asked a skivvy.
'Oh farmer, wherefore is the loo?'
'Your Lordship, it's yon privy.'

The Bishop hurried out of sight
And came back much relieved.
'My gratitude to you, it's right,
And this I have conceived;

A gold chain I will send to you
It will replace the rope I wrecked,
It is the least that I can do.'
But the farmer he looked vexed.

'I am annoyed, it's got my goat,'
(Yes more than just a smidgeon,)
'I wish you hadn't pulled that rope,
You've let out all my pigeons.'

Instruction to a young chef from Cardiff –

'Now open the cheese Caerphilly'.

Happy Nonsense

One fine day in the middle of the night,
Two dead men got up to fight,
Back to back they faced each other,
Drew their swords and shot each other,

One was blind and the other couldn't see,
So they chose a dummy for a referee.
A blind man went to see fair play,
A dumb man went to shout "Hooray!"

A paralysed donkey passing by,
Kicked the blind man in the eye,
Knocked him through a nine inch wall,
Into a dry ditch and drowned them all,

A deaf policeman heard the noise,
And came to arrest the two dead boys,
If you don't believe this story's true,
Ask the blind man he saw it too!

Anon

Q. What is the best tree for a policeman's memorial?
A. A copper beech.

Happier Nonsense

Twas in the month of Liverpool,
In the city of July,
The snow was raining heavily,
The streets were very dry,
The flowers were sweetly singing,
The birds were in full bloom,
As I went down to the cellar
To sweep the upstairs room.

Anon

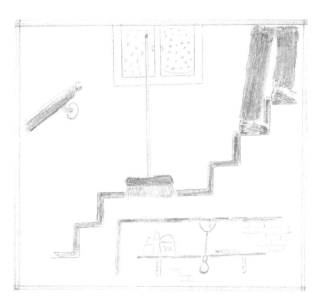

Man finds his wife crying in the kitchen:
Man: What's the matter love?
Wife: I'm homesick.
Man: But this is your home.
Wife: Yes, and I'm sick of it.

(This limerick was sent to me on an email – brilliant.)

There was an old man from Calcutta
Who'd eaten five tons of salt butter.
He grew so fat,
That he needed a hat,
That was fitted with drainpipe and gutter.

(Please note that an attempt was made to find the copyright holder.)

TEACHER: Now, Simon, tell me frankly, do you say prayers before eating?
SIMON: No sir, I don't have to, my Mum is a good cook.

TEACHER: Clyde, your composition on 'My Dog' is exactly the same as your brother's.
Did you copy his?
CLYDE : No, sir. It's the same dog.

Teacher: Sharon, what do you call a person who keeps on talking when people are no longer interested?
Sharon: A teacher.

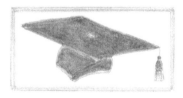

Q: Why did the ace teacher have a cow on the ceiling of her classroom?
A: Because she wanted to give every good child a pat on the head.

More happy Nonsense

As I was going up a stair,
I met a man who wasn't there.
He wasn't there again today.
Oh how I wish he'd go away.

Anon

Bonneyidee

This old man he played one
He played knick-knack on my bomb.....

*(At the primary school I attended as a lad
I heard the following):*

While shepherds washed their
socks by night
All watching BBC,
The angel of the Lord came down
And switched to ITV.

And

We three kings of Leicester square,
selling ladies underwear.
So fantastic, no elastic
Why don't you buy a pair?

O star of wonder, bright to light,
Sit on a box of dynamite!
Light the fuse and you will see
the quickest way to the cemat'ry. (or lavat'ry!)

Also

Good King Wenceslas looked out
in his pink pyjamas,
sliding down the banisters,
eating bad bananas.
Brightly shone the moon last night
over Marks and Spencers,
then a Scotsman came in sight
and he knocked him senseless.

And

Hark, the herald angels sing,
Beecham's pills are just the thing,
They are gentle, meek and mild,
Two for an adult, one for a child.
If you want to go to heaven
You must take a dose of seven,
If you want to go to hell,
Eat the blinkin' box as well…
Hark the herald angels sing
Beecham's pills are just the thing.

Limericks have also inspired me to write poetry – here are a few of my personal favourites.

Famous Limericks

There was a young lady of Riga,
Who rode, with a smile, on a tiger.
They returned from the ride
With the lady inside
And the smile on the face of the tiger.

Anon

A rare old bird is the pelican;
His bill holds more than his belican.
He can hold in his beak
Enough food for a week;
I'm darned if I know how the helican!

Anon

There was an old man of Nantucket
Who kept all his cash in a bucket,
But his daughter, named Nan,
Ran away with a man,
And as for the bucket, Nantucket.

From the 'Princeton Tiger' Author unknown

And this one is a gem:

I sat next to the duchess at tea;
It was just as I feared it would be:
Her rumblings abdominal
Were truly phenomenal,
And everyone thought it was me!

Pres. Woodrow Wilson?

Daytoremember

He passed a copper without a fuss
He passed a cart of hay,
He tried to pass a swerving bus
And then he passed away.

Anon

Delicazoo-en

You'll never bake a Cheatah Cake
No matter how you try,
Though if you take a lion steak
You'll probably just die.

You'll never see a penguin pea
Or wave a camel's carrot,
And if you find some par-boiled Brie
Don't feed it to your parrot.

And never make a tiger sauce
To eat with duck or pheasant,
For tiger sauce contains his claws
Which really isn't pleasant.

You'll not enjoy a foxy pie
Or steamed or roasted pullet,
Though you'll devour a house
louse thigh
Much faster than a bullet.

And if you hated zebra toast
With polar bear jam on it,
Try python's beer, it's sometimes
queer,
But makes a perfect tonic.

So never bake a cheetah cake
(There is a reason why,
You'll find out really what's at stake.)
AND DON'T EAT MONKEY PIE!

(There are a number of poems referring to animals in 'Verse and Worse.' Of all the animals I think the hippo is probably one of the most suited to comedy.)

Little Hoarse

The Hippo is a pretty bird
You'll see him hop and frolic,
And sing like you have never heard
And fit inside a wallet.

He drinks champagne and cups of tea
In trays of six or seven,
That have been brought by land and sea
From Timbuktu or Devon.

And when the hunter comes his way
He hides himself in quarries,
And when the coast is clear again
He feeds on cars and lorries.

He often likes to play a round
Of golf, or bowls, or tennis,
Or stamp a tango on the ground
Which is a fearful menace.

And when he sleeps at end of day
His specs are in his pocket,
His glass eye sits upon the shelf
His teeth soak in a bucket.

His dreams are filled with hairy bears
In uniforms at Clayton,
And snow-capped hills, in night- time airs,
And wakes to eggs and bacon.

This is another poem from Verse and Worse

Epitaph

Here lies John Bunn,
He was killed by a gun.
His name was not Bunn, but Wood,
But Wood would not rhyme with Gun,
But Bunn would.

Anon.

Herpitaph

Here lies Jean Wright,
She was killed by a fright.
Her name was not Wright but Wheel,
But Wheel would not rhyme with fright
But Wheel's right.

Here is an epitaph from 'Verse and Worse'

Who died Feb. 6 1751
Aged45 years & 6 Months

Beneath this smooth stone,
by the bone of his bone,
Sleeps Mr Jonathan Gill.
By lies when alive
This attorney did thrive,
And now that he's dead he lies still.

In the years I spent as a primary school music teacher this song was always a success.

ERECTED TO THE MEMORY TO
THE MEMORY OF MR JONATHAN GILL

Football Crazy

I have a favourite brother,
And his Christian name is Paul.
He's lately joined a football club
For he's mad about football.
He's got two black eyes already
And teeth lost from his gob,
Since Paul became a member of
That terrible football club.

(Chorus)
For he's football crazy,
He's football mad,
The football it has taken away
The little bit o' sense he had,
And it would take a dozen servants
To wash his clothes and scrub,
Since Paul became a member of
That terrible football club.

In the middle of the field, one afternoon,
The captain says, "Now Paul,
Would you kindly take this penalty-kick
Since you're mad about football?"
So he took forty paces backwards,
Shot off from the mark.
The ball went sailing over the bar
And landed in New York.
(Chorus)

His wife, she says she'll leave him
If Paulie doesn't keep
Away from football kicking
At night-time in his sleep.
He calls out 'Pass, McGinty!"
And other things so droll
Last night he kicked her out of bed
And swore it was a goal!
(Chorus)

James Curran?

Someone's been taking liberties again.

The wonders of
the Mini-verse

Greatest Gape

My deft Macaw likes aspirins
From tubs or tubes or packs or tins
And now I've looked there's none at all
Because my parrot's ate* 'em all.

(pronounced 'et')

The Yearnings of J. L. Bird

I am described by all my friends
As an exemplary man.
I work for naught for many hours
And give help when I can.
I do not smoke and seldom drink
Or mess around with women,
And all of this is going to change
When I get out of prison.

The newly released prisoner realised that the friendliest people were sometimes to be found behind bars.

Literally a Princess

The consummate works of Jane Austin
Those novels that readers get lost in.
Her Stoke on Trent style
Beats Dahl by a mile,
With insight and judgement are bostin'

Upshot

I'd have liked to been a fly on the wall, at the circus interview when they were trying to fill a vacancy caused by the dismissal of the human cannonball. After twenty unsuccessful applicants it is believed that Billy Smart turned to his chief manager and said that the trouble was that – these days he couldn't get people of the right calibre.

2.

Non Clod-Hopper

They say that when you're in a garden,
You are much nearer to God.
But if you fall over
A big patch of clover
You'll end up much nearer the sod.

Out-Clapped

And have you heard about –
The Italian lady's dilapidated Vauxhall –
She calls it her
Caverlieria Rusticana.

A level you're history

'The Greek Olympiad begat
multiple field events such as the
hurling of weighty conical objects.'
Discuss.

(Heard by an adult passing a child's bedroom door)

"If you're happy and you know it get the clap,
If you're …….."

Riverthick

Cleopatra believed that the Nile
Contained a benign crocodile,
She went for a swim
Was torn limb from limb,
And her spirit is still in denial.

Pater-retaP

He came from a family of talented acrobats
so naturally his father was an excellent
role model.

Scullery made

I view the sliced beetroot that stains
The lino near the kitchen door.
Consuming the remaining gains
And now I'm red in tooth and floor.

Salutation to the nice lady on the bacon machine in Sainsbury's

Nice to see you
To see you slice.

The next poem is again quoted from
'Verse and Worse.'

Nursery Rhyme

Doctor Bell fell down a well
And broke his collar-bone.
Doctors should attend the sick
And leave the well alone.

(?) Eighteenth Century

Ringing Success

Doctor Bell a cell did cage,
He made it all alone,
And inventors in the modern age
Have made the cell a phone.

Sticky Business

Doctor Blue as wise men do
He plaited hemp and rape,
He added lots of pots of glue
And invented cellotape.

This poem is another poem from 'Verse and Worse'

A Rhyme

(Inscribed on a pint pot)

There are several reasons for drinking,
And one has just entered my head;
If a man cannot drink while he's living
How the hell can he drink when he's dead?

Anon

Amnesiboozer

Forgive Balid Cruz,
For the fact that he does,
Drink lager and wine by the flagon.
For I've heard on my phone,
He has problems at home,
And his wife, it is known, is a dragon.

Imbiberess

And forgive Maxis Crewe,
As actors will do,
Drinks absinthe and often gets plastered.
Her life's not enriched,
As pregnant she hitched,
To a man, who's a word, I've not mastered.

Dodgeredo

And then there's old Pap,
Who's seen with his cap,
In the pub, as he sits, on his throne.
He's full of good cheer
As he swigs at his beer
And he's sometimes been known to go home.

Please note:
Some of this was written in a pub
But it's not ingenious.

Jagman

A mad lad who came from Stotfold,
Whilst building a tree house I'm told,
He fell off a ladder,
Which just made him madder,
So he killed a large stag on the road.

(The last line of the above is factually incorrect – poetic licence.)

A blind man went a long Wagner opera with his guide dog. He enjoyed the show and someone asked him what the dog thought. He said he didn't like Wagner he preferred Bach.

Snogger

Ewan kissed me by the spring
And Bernard by the pool,
And Lenny thinks I'll wear his ring!
(He must think I'm a fool.)

I'll kiss Tom whose lousy cold
To me to germs exposes,
But Mark is camp and wet and old
And he has halitosis.

I've kissed some very handsome men
Like Mick who comes from Wick,
But if Martin kisses me again
I think that I'll be sick.

Deaquefied

An indian from the old wild west
Was riding on a train.
His name was 'Big Chief Sitting Bull'
His squaw was 'Little Flame.'

He sent his squaw to fetch a drink
Three times it all befell,
On third return she said, 'Me can't,
Um paleface sitting on well.'

These two limericks are from 'Verse and Worse'

There was a young lad of St Just
Who ate apple pie 'til he bust;
It wasn't the fru-it
That caused him to do it,
What finished him off was the crust.

Anon

There was an old man from Darjeeling,
Who travelled from London to Ealing
It said on the door,
'Please do not spit on the floor'
So he carefully spat on the ceiling.

Anon

Tell me, why is it that when I go upstairs on a bus, the
nutter always comes and sits by me?

Graffiti from the back of a gravestone

Here lies my wife.
When I cease to be
(My trouble and strife)
Let me lie with thee.

And someone else added –
Go get thee gone
For like life before
You'll wreck my sleep,
With deaf'ning snore.

3.

Look it's the ....

Gardener's Revenge

Last night I killed my cheating wife,
And laid her 'neath the cabbage patch.
(I know that doesn't scan or rhyme)
But peace at last! And she's sub-lime.

(Cabbages grow well in soil with plenty of lime.)

We'llkipperwhelkum

Epitaph to a corrupt fish merchant-

In a sea of guilt he floundered.

The following five poems are from 'Verse and Worse'

The Budding Bronx

Der spring is sprung
Der grass is riz
I wonder where den boidies is?

Der littke boids is on der wing,
Ain't dat absoid?
Der little wings is on the boid!
Anon (The Bronx, New York)

There was an old fellow from Lympne*
Who married three wives at one time;
When asked: 'Why the third?'
He replied, 'One's absurd;
And bigamy, Sir, is a crime.'

(*pronounced Lime)

Longing

I wish I was a little grub
With whiskers round my tummy,
I'd climb into a honey-pot
And make my tummy gummy.

Anon

Epigram from the French

Sir, I admit your general rule,
That every poet is a fool:
But you yourself may serve to show it,
That every fool is not a poet.

Alexander Pope

Definition of Camping - Loitering within tent.

Sign from a Camping Shop Window

Now is the discount
of our winter tents.

Ignoreblissance

See the happy moron,
He doesn't give a damn.
I wish I was a moron –
My God I think I am!

Limerick

The writings of Joseph Von Elevent
Were crazy and mainly irrelevent,
Of his musings galore
Like 'Mad dogs for the poor!'
I'm really not sure what the hell 'e meant.

Thinnerick

Whilst slimming a young girl – Evette
Lost weight by much more than was set,
She said she was glad to,
But found that she had to,
Run round in the shower to get wet.

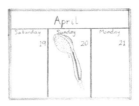

Let us spray.

Hymnerick

There was a young girl in the choir
Whose voice rose higher and higher
Till it reached such a height
It was clear out of sight,
And they found it next day on the spire.

Anon

Felineabhor

Of dogs and cats I refer to the latter,
Dumping and depositing offensive matter,
Causing anger and garden ruin,
And not a fit subject for a poo-em.

Upstartitis

'Tis dogs delight to bark and bite
And little girls to sing.
And if you sit on a red hot brick
It's the sign of an early spring.

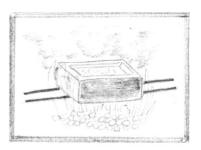

*After the repeated incidents with the au pair and the next
door neighbour, the enraged the lady placed the red hot
brick on the front seat of her husband's BMW.*

Zany Views

Denilebattle

The boy stood on the burning deck,
Whence all were in retreat,
His bloodshot eyes were filled with tears
His shoes were filled with feet.

Then up and spake our Captain Bold
'Oh good lad have a care.'
But Captain Bold, his heart was cold,
He'd lost his teddy bear.

The boy still stood though abandon ship
Was called out on the wreck,
But no one had a clue his shoes,
Were glued on to the deck.

Then fifty rats jumped from below
Came tumbling on the deck
And sailors all did hear their call
'We're out of 'ere, by heck!'

Now the captain grabbed the lad
And pulls him by the ear,
And they escape the burning place
The sailors they all cheer.
(Well two of them)

Now fighting wars is quite insane
And stupid we'd agree,
And here's my thanks, it was a game,
We're watching on TV.

The boy was on the burning deck,
The pride of all the fleet.
His weary eyes now show surprise
And he still has his feet.

Singing in the Rhine

There was a young lady from Gage,
Sang Wagner quite loud in a rage,
And the outcome you see,
Was such high frequency
That it cracked a large mirror on stage.

Hit-the-deck

I wish I had not bought a ticket,
For the diva was plainly not with-it,
The donkey then threw,
On the stage his do-do
And then *Beecham he quipped "What a critic!"

Beecham was a famous conductor.
Here's another poem from 'Verse and Worse'

The Bloody Orkneys

This bloody town's a bloody cuss
No bloody trains, no bloody bus,
And no one cares for bloody us
In bloody Orkney.

The bloody roads are bloody bad,
The bloody folks are bloody mad,
They'd make the brightest bloody sad,
In bloody Orkney.

All bloody clouds, and bloody rains,
No bloody kerbs, no bloody drains,

The Council's got no bloody brains,
In bloody Orkney.

Everything's so bloody dear,
A bloody bob, for bloody beer,
And is it good? – no bloody fear,
In bloody Orkney.

The bloody 'flicks' are bloody old,
The bloody seats are bloody cold,
You can't get in for bloody gold
In bloody Orkney.

The bloody dances make you smile,
The bloody band is bloody vile,
It only cramps your bloody style,
In bloody Orkney.

No bloody sport, no bloody games,
No bloody fun, the bloody dames
Won't even give their bloody names
In bloody Orkney.

Best bloody place is bloody bed,
With bloody ice on bloody head,
You might as well be bloody dead,
In bloody Orkney.

There's nothing greets your bloody eye
But bloody sea and bloody sky,
'Roll on demob!' we bloody cry
In bloody Orkney.

*The above poem has been attributed to a Captain Hamish
Blair, RN, who is said to have been stationed at Scapa Flow
during WWII.*

Crank Designs

The property was advertised
On an upmarket Google site,
Well positioned and secluded
Though it didn't seem quite right.

The framework of the building
Was solid beyond belief.
Though a entirely free of gilding
Which we viewed with great relief.

There was no double glazing
Or roof parts or a door.
Though the view it was amazing
And grass grew on the floor.

The local farmer's livestock could
Prefer to wander there.
And swooping from a local wood
Two barn owls came to stare.

(But we bought it because)

It really was important to.
Impress our sham 'close' friends
That's why we saw the project through
To renovate Stonehenge.

There is now an obsession with mobile phone, computers etc. Sitting, reading as usual, in an empty room in a pub when in walked a young man, talking on his mobile. He said something showing his anger and then threw his mobile on the floor and proceeded to stamp heavily on it several times. He stopped and the mobile started ringing – with a dazed expression he lifted up the phone and said 'Oh it's you'.

Google – who needs it? I only have to ask the wife.

(Sung to the tune of 'Home on the Range')

Homophonia

Oh give me a phone,
Made in plastic and chrome,
With a qwerty keyboard for my play,
Where my thumbs it's averred,
Will fire up in a blur,
And the time will slip by 'til I'm grey.
I'll drone on the phone,
And be thrilled as a dog with a bone,
and I'll twitter and tweet,
with the folks I'll ne'er meet,
and all of my cash has been blown.

Oh give me an app,
That does not need a strap,
And a tablet that's not made to suck,
And glasses that kind,
That get into your mind,
And providers that'll give me no truck.
I'll email (so chaste)
By employing the old cut and paste,
And when I've paid for broadband,
With an arm and a hand,
I'll adjust the broad band round my waist.

Frankly it amazes me that some lads when they're out
with a stunning, vivacious young lady actually prefer to
look at their phones. I fully support those who upon
seeing him go to the gents, have sometimes dumped
their friend's phone in his beer.

4.

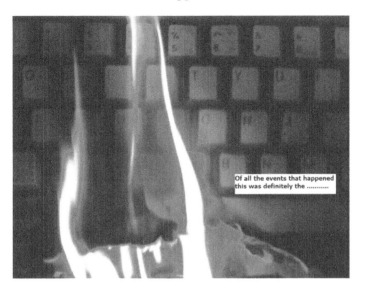

Of all the events that happened this was definitely the ....

Crematakeyboard

When I was on line
The other day.
Visiting sites
Where you don't have to pay.
Joined in a chat room
And typed away,
But then it dawned on me
That they were all gay!

And that's why I'm about to;
Sling and torch the router
Because it will be fun
And I'll burn the computer
(Clickerty clickerty click)
And get out in the sun!

My eyes are now square
And my nerves are frayed
My backside is melded
to the chair I'm afraid
I'm an inside man
As I'm trapped in the shade
And my power point plan
Has crashed and decayed.

And that's why I'm about to;
Sling and torch the router
And give thanks when it's done
And I'll re-program the computer
(Clickerty clickerty click)
With a gun!

My waistline is growing
'Cause the fat it is storing
My blood pressure's rising
And the migraine is soaring
My mind's apoplectic
Because U-tube is boring
And you can't tell the web sites
from the carpet or flooring.

And that's why I'm about to;
Sling and torch the router
For all the trouble and strife
And I'll shred the computer
(Clickerty clickerty click)
–*sound effect; crunching metal*
And get a life!

Aggressive driving is now commonplace on British
roads – the stories I could tell – don't get me started!

Ticketitus

A policeman pulls over a speeding car
And says,
'I clocked you doing 80 miles an hour.'
'Well officer,' the driver replies
'I'll tell the truth and not disguise
The fact I'd set the cruise control at sixty
And believe me I'm not celebrating
But perhaps your gun needs calibrating?'

In the passenger seat the wife
Who has a tongue as sharp as any knife
Says, 'Listen, for on a number of occasions
to me you've made it very clear
this car has no cruise control dear.'

And as the officer writes out the ticket
And the driver thinks where he can stick it
The driver leans over to the wife
and with a growl
He spews out a put down – something foul.

But the wife demurely smiles
and with wicked fire
says, 'Well your speed
could have been even higher,
Be thankful for your little protector
You know, your handy radar detector.'

As the officer writes out another note
The driver says
'I'll ram that tongue right down your throat,'
but the policeman who is now staring,
says, 'I notice sir that you're not wearing
A seat belt (an oft committed crime)
And that's an automatic fine.'

The driver now of a less confident mind
Says, 'Well I had it on my shoulder
But seeing you coming over
I slipped it off its clip and sprocket,
So I could get my licence
out o'my back pocket.'

The wife now speaks, she shows no fear,
she says
'But you never wear your seat belt dear.'
The driver now can hardly breathe,
His very being starts to seethe,
His face now a purplish hue,
He says ' Be quiet or I'll murder you!'

The officer says
'Does your husband always
talk to you this way ma'am?'
Thinking –
'The road hog's crap at keeping calm!'
Says she,
' I can see the way you're thinking
But no, ... well ....
Only when he's been drinking.'

....traffic light? What traffic light?!

Misvisage

I was in my office
having just visited
The Isle of Dogs, Eastend,
Reviewing the winners
Of the regional heats of
Grotesque face
Golden Gob awards.
(A sort of Miss World of the gargoyles)
In preparation for the finals.
England South East had
produced an interesting tied result i.e.
The Minner twins: Harold and Albert
Who were actually not related.

Having printed and cropped
One example of each of the contestants'
most contorted faces,
They were now staring out
from my notice board
As I pondered:

Minner 'nd Minner, on the wall
Who is the scariest of Millwall.

Short notes on pets that can perform simple household tasks

How useful it would be if
As well as the obvious benefits
Your cat could say- do the ironing.
Or the budgie could post a letter.
I'd prefer a ferret that could clean your car.
You know he'd be able to reach
all those parts the vacuum couldn't.
Or even a rabbit that that did the dusting.
Dogs would of course feature highly in this
As their benevolent nature
and innate intelligence
would suit them to many tasks,
Such as cleaning the windows or making soup.
The male dogs might prefer the manly jobs like
mowing the lawn or mending a window.
And the house-proud bitches
could do the washing up,
But that's entirely up to them.
I wouldn't insist...
and I'd do things for them in return
Like throwing a stick or buying a tin of food,
We'd just be helping one another.

Dedicated to the radio 3 programme 'The Verb' and particularly the voice of Ian Macmillan.

Hippex

With life it's hard to get to grips
And work at my relationships,
But Aunties now have tripped on stones
And damaged fragile pelvic bones,
So cares I have (and things to fix)
As well as my relations' hips.

Poem to the Great Unwashed

Without a shower,
I'm saving power
And cash and time he thinks,
But I've been near him
And had to breathe in
So I say
I don't care what he thinks
It's really a case of
Evil to him
Who evil stinks.

Hoof hearted?

5.

.... every day.

Incommunicado

The Lord is my iPhone;
I shall dark font.
He maketh me to scroll down
in streamed pixels
He tweeteth me beside
the sync portal.
He diverteth my call: He selphieth me
In the paths of frequencies for his
games' sake.
Yea, though I swipe through the
warehouse of the carphone of death,
I will fear no iPod: for iCloud
art with me;
Thy blog and thy app they comfort me.
Thou installest a cable before me
in the presence of my accessories
Thou anointest my Tech with foil:
my hub runneth over.
Surely twooshness and cookies
shall follow me
all the days of my swipe:
And I will text in the house
of O2 for ever.

Miss Cellany

Squirrelled Away

You may have met them,
I refer to the Somairni family
Formerly of Abu Dhabi
But now proprietor of a locally famous
Michelin star restaurant
In a converted farmhouse near Baxterley.
The chef Abdul Somairni.
In the game season
Prepared stew for the freezer
Using some skinned squirrels.
(Aka River Cottage)
But mostly some plucked crows.
This proved fortuitous as on one occasion
A coach broke down on an adjacent meadow
Disgorging fifty very hungry prison inmates.
They having been travelling for six hours
And the coach driver having slavishly
followed his sat nav.
They raided the freezer and
The felons feasted.
And thus the occurrence was reported
In the local Newsrag
Concluding:

Never in a field of human convicts,
Was so much bowled,
By Somairni,
Via crow stew.

And on a more philosophical note:
(Let's not put Descartes before the horse.)

I think therefore I am.
I am pink therefore I am Spam.

There was a young lady named Bright
Whose speed was far faster than light;
She went out one day,
In a relative way,
And returned on the previous night.
A, H, Reginald Buller?

(Warning this poem contains gory images.)

6.

Outside the cinema there was a ……..

Night out

'Quarkdom of Skin-Freaks'
Was not only the first 007/Zombie film ever made
but probably the last.
I had been dragged along to our local fleapit
by Maggy, my partner.
A good sort but a bit of an alchy.
She always snook in cans of Extra Strength Lager
in her handbag,
Which I judiciously refused.
'Oh go on, you know you want to,'
She propositioned me,
But no way.
I can see it now – being stopped on the way home
(Slurred voice – police siren)
'Good Consternoon Afterble'
I can hear the cell door closing….
Back at the Multisex –
Gratuatous violence, hacked off limbs
and gory mondeos filled the screen,
It weren't my cuppa tea,
But then those of the visceral enlightenment
filling the other seats,
should be getting their money's worth.
Well that's what I reckoned,
No I never did like creepy films
since that day I saw Pinochio
turn into a pizzahouse,

But I sat there all the same
'Cause I was hoping for a little favour later...
(James Blond gives blokes ideas)
Anyway it didn't seem long 'til we were leaving
and that's when it occurred to me
while passing the hamster food counter,
that I was feeling as you might expect,
Like the 007 gulpdown ....
shaken – but not slurred.

Cracking Up

Have you heard the one about the drug pusher
who has been committed
for a court appearance.
He will be hauled up at Stafford assizes,
in front of His Lordship Justice Derror.
The prosecution plan portray him
not as hero in
the local community but as a bit of a
downer and outer.
The whole thing will be sorted out in time
one way or another by
trial an' Derror.

Lord Justice Wigg,

I would like to propose a new word for the OED

'Tercha'

Commonly heard in England
when you're out for a country walk.

You are apprehensive
due to the approaching stranger's,
off the leash, slightly aggressive, large dog.

The owners will often attempt
to reassure you
with the time honoured:

"He wont-tercha."

Mindless

Wandering through an estate
I came across Whitehouse Road
which I was about to enter
when I noticed the sign 'Residents only'.

However ignoring this I proceeded to No. 24
home of Russel Grant
which had the sign ' Prescience Only'.

Just across the road a tradesman's van
specializing in car body repairs
which had the legend 'Pressi – dents only.'

It occurred to me that The Whitehouse,
Washington DC probably has an allotted
car parking space labelled Presidents Only.

Hymenopera

I am pondering whether to write a singing drama
based on the environmental plight of bees and wasps.
Naturally it will include a wordless buzzing chorus,
many aerial curving melodies
with a flower duet or two.
I'll probably hive off the task
of writing the libretto
and the finale will be momentous,
since that will be when the
fat lady stings.

(My mother told me the following alledgedly true story.)

Absolutely Trilling

About fifty years ago my father was entrusted
with the job of clearing the house
of my recently
departed great aunt Patty.
More importantly perhaps he was intent
on finding the money my aunt had hidden.
After some determined searching
nothing was found.
It was then decided that my father
would attend a séance
to contact her departed spirit.
No contact was made with my aunt,
but the medium did make contact
with my aunt's budgie –
details of the money's location were relayed
and they turned out to be true.

Spandiculous

After having a minor tiff with his partner Mike, a mature college student, was walking along a beach in California when he came upon a bottle tossing in the waves. After some effort he managed to remove the cork. Immediately smoke poured out of the bottle and (you've guessed it) a genie appeared.

'At last!' thundered the Genie, sending out a huge shock wave which sent Mike cartwheeling across the sand. Mike picked himself up and the Genie said, 'Greetings master, you have rendered me a great service; in return I will grant you one wish. It would have been three but everyone's cutting their budgets these days.'

Mike replied – 'Well I don't fly and I'd like to go on holiday to Hawaii, so could you build me a bridge?'
    The Genie paused and thought for a few seconds. 'That's quite a large undertaking, master, is there anything else that would do instead?'
Now it was Mike's turn to think. 'I'd really like to know why when my lady gets upset she says 'No' when she really means 'Yes.''
    The Genie gave a wry smile and putting his arm around Mike's shoulder said,
    'That bridge? Was that a one lane or two?'

Duckndive

I was swapping jokes with a gentleman from
Cambridge – his was better than mine.
He said –
'My father threw me in, for my first swimming lesson
at the age of three –
it took me ten minutes to get out of the sack'.

7.

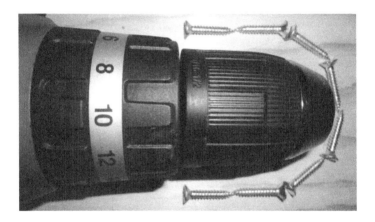

There was definitely......

My son at the time this was written was happily
purchasing machine tools to start a house renovating
business. Only the best tools would do namely 'De Walt'
bought from the catalogue 'Screwfix'.

Youscrew

Our Nirvana
Who art at Screwfix
Hallowed De Walt by name.
Thy catalogues come
Thy drills be spun, with mirth,
As it is on page seven.
Give us this day our safety vests
And supply us our lens glasses
As we survive those who smash glass around us
And lead us not into temptation
And so deliver us from Homebase.
For thine is the pantheon
The power tools and the Allen keys,
For fellers more clever than
Car-men.

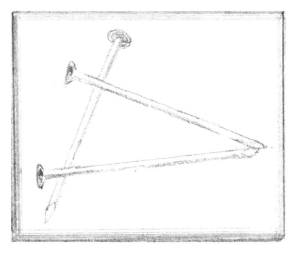

Metal dowels

Rab C Nesbit

I work at Mactavishes
Down Canine Lane
Aye, in the dogs' hame
We have three pregnant poodles
Two of which produced
only last night.
Now you might well be askin y'self..
(Mob phone rings)
Scuse me, Yes, hellooo,
(listens) Wonderful. Noo problem.
Sorry, have t'rush
We've a few more mouths t'feed
Just need t, pick up
another tin o'Tescos doggy pudding
from this wonderful supermarket
I mustnee pause for thought
For you know what they say
At Mactavishes'.......
Every Poodle whelps.

Meet the Hoodys

Robin, Will and Johners were members
of the Hoody family.
Maybe you've heard of them
They're famous because they have
an arboreal interest bordering on mania.
Trees fill the lives of these reprobates
Though tree fellers they are not.
Robin is the most recognisable
He's the one with a bow….
In his hair.

Every day rising early at 11am
they (being peckish) visit the Friar Truck
(the proprietor being no less than
Omaha Sherriff
formerly of Snottingham)
for a bacon sandwich-hazel baguette
Before proceeding to the local forest
With their chipper mate Douglas Fir
Who is often axed along.

Poor Johners (the elder of the three)
looks sad,
Having been jilted at the altar
by his sick amour
she left him in the larch
pining away.
Life can certainly deal you a poor hand.

(Somewhat in reverse
Robin's seen a little too much
of his lady love recently
with her 24/7 last week
You could say he's a little maid marionated.)

In t'woodland archery features now
And after a harrowing target practise
They proceed to carve
'Acorns rule, Oak eh?'
In plane English for all to see
on the nearest beech.

A little burglary may follow
Anne Robinson's house
Was the last one.
Though they give most of the proceeds
to a German charity thus
Robbing the witch
To give to the Ruhr.

It's a fact that Robin aspires
to become a follower of
A secular society-brotherhood
The Menin.
He fancies dressing in the vermin robes
undergoing some farcical initiation ritual
before being ordained
into the lower order of the Menintites.

They finish their day
And I wont palm you off
In front of the box
Would that I could leaf it alone.

Hire Perches

A friend of mine had ghostly experience.
He related to me the story of how
on several occasions
he had woken to find the apparition
of the slightly dimmed vivid
colours of a giant McCaw
sitting on the bed rail.
He was not disturbed unduly by the vision
until it spoke to him,
in a voice similar to that of one
of the snooker commentators on the television
and proceeded to charge, like a bull,
up and down the room,
finally disappearing through a wall.

I don't know for certain but this may
be an example of the parrotnormal.

Profprofane

Excuse my sodding French but
This ruddy watch is useless,
Hope it's got a smegging guarantee
I don't know about you but
That's the last time I buy something
from the Betterswear catalogue.

The following is based on a true incident.

Elevating Situation

An aged lady Margaret Brown,
At Waldorf suite in New York town
Was descending in the lift alone
The box now slowed, with braking tone
And in walked three unnerving men.
Their looks were grim and threatening then
With seeming spite, to Marg they turned around
And one says, 'Ok Grandma, HIT THE GROUND!'
So down she hastens to comply
But to her aid the men reply
By helping her back to her feet
And courteously (to her relief)
She was assisted out and to a taxi cab
It was unthinkable that anyone they'd stab.
(later)
Mag never saw the men again
She looked out often but in vain.
And when she left where she had stayed
She found the bill had all been paid,
And signed below (not camp or girly)
Was the name of Eddie Murphy.

A spotty teenager was caught by his mum with his pointing finger poked up his nasal cavity.
'Stoppit,' she said.
He replied, 'But mum if someone has to give me mouth to nose resuscitation - I'm clearing the way.'

*(David Attenborough voice – wasp in high
magnification fills screen)*

Sideswipe

Vespula Engrossopola,
Known commonly in India
as the Challalii - literally fat wasp.
Never excavates a nest below ground as..
(Wasp stings DA)
Off Camera – 'Ow The little......' (Controls voice.)
.... 'do his British equivalents
or indeed raid the nests of other smaller insects
due to its generous proportions.
It is therefore never referred to
In its native land at least as
a burrower or a slender bee.'

(Offstage sound – shoe hitting rock)

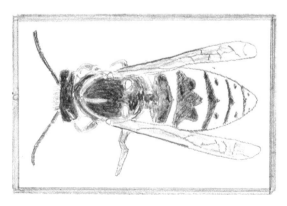

Wily antisocial stinging predator.

Two ageing poet lovers meet

He said – She said

He – I drink in your pink chin.
She thinks - Both of them?

She – You fill up my séances
He thinks – It was love at first fright.

He – A face that launched a thousand ships.
She thinks – More like a paunch
that braced a thousand slips.

She – Your teeth in the firmament do dwell like stars.
He thinks – Why yes they come out at night.

He – Your lips, so luscious, are like the petals.
She thinks – Bicycle petals.

She – You are a fine figure of a man,
my Lochinvar.
He thinks – A pity it's a figure 8.

He – You walk in beauty like the night.
She thinks – But I would lose the cape and fangs.

She – Fly me to the moon.
He thinks – Where else would I take an alien?

Toothless

The following conversation took place on a trip to the dentist.
After having my teeth polished with the brush attachment
I commented that –
'Now I know what a drain feels like when Dyno Rod have been.'
To which the dentist replied without pause –
'Oh no, if we were Dyno Rod we'd have gone in from the other end.'

'He's pregnant?!'

Manysicked Slumbercatch

Before we were married Chris (short for Christine) and I went on a holiday to Sweden . We travelled in my battered old mini to Newcastle upon Tyne and had a pleasant 'flat as a millpond' sea-crossing of about 24 hours to Gothenburg.

The holiday was largely uneventful. We camped and walked and visited Oslo by train, where food was quite expensive. I do remember one morning when we woke to a kind of zipping sound going down the side of the tent. This turned out to be the local small birds which were perching on the apex of the tent and then sliding down the fabric and having a great time. We also saw two ten year old girls in swimming costumes playing on a slide in about 18" of water, in a lake, splashing around and having a lot of fun. Thinking it a good idea we ventured in only to find the water to be near freezing point. (Note: Swedish ladies are no wimps.)

On the last day we needed to return to Gothenburg but found that the car wouldn't start. This was probably due to the 'headlights on' Swedish law. So, needing a push we asked some burly Swedish campers for help. They positively enjoyed the experience and shouted to each other happily.

As the car started, one of them yelled 'Fromstat' and the others all cheered. (Apparently this meant 'flying start.')

As we neared Gothenburg I realised that we were running out of fuel which I promptly forgot about until the engine died on the quayside. I departed with the water container to buy fuel leaving Chris wondering what would happen if the queue started to embark. Luckily I was back in time. On board the ferry all went well except that I managed to irreparably break my glasses – something that was to prove unhelpful later on.

At about 3am that night the weather deteriorated somewhat. Probably about a force 4 – 5 gale resulting in much rolling. I don't know if you have experienced a sea journey like this one but if you haven't then perhaps I could explain a little – the ship rolls (as you face the bows ie. the way the ship is travelling) from right to left, at the same time as it climbs waves it rolls from front to rear. Rolling also takes place on either diagonal sometimes veering unpredictably from one to the other. Combine all three and the result of this was fairly obvious for a couple of landlubbers like Chris and myself. Heave ho.

Inside the cabin strange things began to occur – the bunk bed (hinged down the long side) that I had recently vacated began to move up and down of its own accord. At the time this mystified me but I soon realised that we have this built in perception that the 'walls don't move' which meant that to my mind the walls were always vertical, thus a bed that behaved in this way was decidedly odd.

Now we became very seasick and decided to leave the cabin. Someone advised us to move down to the lower decks where the motion of the boat was less but this didn't help so we climbed to the passenger deck level where the fresh air and being able to see the horizon did make a small difference. We stayed there for the rest of the night talking to other passengers and looking forward to being on dry land again.

Some hours later we were summoned to the car deck to disembark only to find that the car was still refusing to behave itself - so Chris got out and we both pushed the mini towards a ramp, on which I bump started the engine. The ramp had a 'No Walking ' sign on it, but a member of the ship's crew, with something of a belittling look, gave Chris the nod to carry on and run down it to catch up.

On dry land again we decided not to camp but instead to go for a B & B where I had the oddest sensation whist walking up the staircase – the steps and walls moved as if I was still on the ship.

In the room we were soon bedded down in two single beds, feeling grateful to be back safely on land we were very soon asleep.

The next thing I remember was having a worrying dream that I was back on board. Half sleepwalking I made for the door, was through it and on the landing hearing the lock snap closed behind me before I realised what I was doing. Fortunately I was wearing pyjamas.

Now slightly disorientated I wasn't absolutely sure which room I'd come from. Trying the door to the right I found it was open and walking in found a stranger, fortunately fast asleep, in my bed. Oops wrong room. Exit stage left pronto. Now certain which room I needed I decided to go downstairs. Just then another resident came up the stairs. I don't remember what I said to him but he went away with a rather surprised look on his face.

Heading downstairs feeling my way down a dark corridor I reached into a side room and flipped on a light switch. Almost at my feet there appeared a small dog, lying on its back, tongue hanging out fortunately totally relaxed. It then occurred to me that I would probably give the lady owner a heart attack if I carried on, so with the brain finally working I decided to ring the front door bell. Chris was still asleep as I was readmitted to the room.

Next morning over breakfast the lady owner asked us if we'd slept well - to which the reply was – yes eventually.

Two days or so later we arrived home where I distinctly remember Chris's father commenting that both of us *still* looked green.

Vatertherapy

It happened on a Polynesian isle,
No high blown story to beguile,
The strong Wakiki lived within his tribe
And he had a bad luck we can describe
(Though scamp he was, he hadn't sinned)
His suffered with the most appalling wind.
Which all agreed was way beyond the limit
When you were caught and held within it.

His friends then found a bottle on the shore
They didn't know the liquid that it bore
It had a pungent, aromatic smell
And it looked green as far as they could tell.
It seemed to offer hope of cure
If it could pass o'er Wakiki's jaw
So they held him down and dosed him up
Poured down his throat cup after cup.

Imagine though (it made them curse)
It only made the smell get worse!
So to the village elder made their way
And asked him all at once if he could say.
What was the cure for this affliction
And he replied in clearest diction.

'You lads have tried to mend this fault,
I'm pleased though that you've called a halt
We'd all be better off if it was found
To cure Wakiki's pong and steamship sound.
I'll not berate you any longer

You see...

Absinthe makes the fart grow stronger.'

Needlegiver

A lady from a wealthy family, who often finds
herself travelling long distances
on motorways, drives the family Rolls Royce,
which is a very easy car to operate.
Driving for her becomes tedious and vaguely boring
and so holding the steering wheel
with one finger she proceeds to knit.

One stretch of motorway proves particularly empty
and without the lady
noticing the car's speed increases to near 90 miles an
hour. Inevitably a police
car pulls alongside with the window down.
With a sigh of annoyance the lady
winds down her window whilst reducing her
speed slightly.
The policeman shouts loudly 'Pull over!'
The reply was, 'No - Socks!'

*My uncle was so strong he could take two pokers
and a reel of wire and knit a fence.*

89

(The song below was very popular at my primary school.)

Drill Ye Tarriers

Every morning at seven o'clock
There's twenty tarriers a workin at the rock
Then the boss comes along and he says, 'Keep still
And come down heavy on the cast iron drill.'

Chorus:

And drill, ye tarriers, drill!
Drill, ye tarriers, drill!
And it's work all day for the sugar in your tea,
Down beyond the railway!
So drill ye tarriers drill,
And blast and fire.

Our new foreman name it was John McCann
And say by God, he was a blame mean man.
Last week a premature blast went off
And a mile in the air went big Jim Goff.

Chorus:

Next time the payday came around
Jim Goff a dollar short was found!
'What for?' he asked, and he got this reply
'You were docked for the time you were up in the sky.'

Chorus:

El Parodiso

(My friend Rob introduced me to the poem 'Stopping by Woods' by Robert frost.)

8.

A famous golfer......

Woodstop

Whose woods are these I think I know.
His locker's in the room below;
These clubs should not be sitting here
But whose they are I do not know.

The club attendant's coming near
And he must think it rather queer
That I look on the table's hoard
Whilst I am tense and waiting here.

He gives his wiry head a shake
To ask (as if!) there's some I'd take
And would my skin begin to creep
To think there's any move I'd make!

The woods are shiny, arched, not cheap,
But on their owner I'll not cheat,
For I'll be honest and be brief
I'm just a poem pinching thief.

Golfers in Afghanistan need a lot of balls.

Dippa's Song

Bud beer's at 'The Spring'
And daze at the morn.
Bar-links at seven?
The Pils guide's brew-curled.
The dark's on the rim,
The pale's robbed the horn.
Grog's on 'til 'leven-
All's light with the world.

Lebanese Degenderate

The chief defect of Zaida Zing
Was needing of a sex change thing,
So then she reasoned - in her prime
And booked the operation's time.
Phoenicians of the utmost fame
Were called at once, and called by name
They answered, 'Yes,' (upon their knees)
There is no cure for boy disease,
Zaida will very soon be Fred.'
Her parents stood about in dread
Lamenting this untimely threat,
When Zaida with her greatest breath
Cried, 'Oh my friends not scorning, see,
My gender means a lot to me,
And all my human mind requires,
Is that all loud abuse retires.'

Shook-up Shakespeare

Let me not to marriage of two dykes
Admit impoverishments. Life is not life
If sep'rate when the high vacation finds,
Nor blends with the ground coffee to aid strife,
Not white! It is for ever fixed dark,
To look on software and be never shaken.
And in the start of every camping lark,
Which trips alone in woe would not be taken.
Likes not Thai food? Though noisy chops and steak,
Within their fav'rite modern rest'raunts soon:
Life alters not with Mel's long shifts and breaks,
But bears it out for both until the hols of June.
If they be in Glasgow, in studio improved
They always sit, where no bear ever moved.

Car registration – LE581AN.

9.

Newcastle under Lyme

It must be ....

(The next poem was written when I was looking after my aging mum in Porthill and I had to go shopping twice a week in Newcastle Under Lyme.)

Castle Leaver

I must go down for the cheese again,
and the slice of ham that I fry,
And all I ask, is a scribbled list
and a car to carry me by,
And the traders call and the old town hall
and the old bells ringing,
And the video man and the butcher's van
and hear the clubbers swinging.

I must go down for the cheese again,
for a rag on the shelf that lies,
For a birdseed ball, from a market stall
that sold those old mince pies;
And at Brampton halt, the rail's at fault
and the old train's vanished,
And I hurried on while the sun shone,
cause the old girl's famished.

I must go down for the cheese again,
to the assistant's weary life,
With a working grudge, and a 'Ta shug,'
from a face like netted tripe;
And the tills ring and the tannoys sing
and the milk's all from clover,
And time's flew, for the tea's due,
now the short trek's over.

Footballer's Wife

Shall I compare thee to a
weathered rake?
Thou art less useful and
more delicate:
New gowns do cause the
normal press affray,
And lacking is your common
sense to date:
Sometimes too high the height
of cashpile flies,
And oft is our fooled compr'hension
dimmed:
And every change of hair your
spouse decides,
Compares to rounded haystack pile
now strimmed;
But thy eternal blandness shall
not fade,
Nor lose the measure of those
breasts you bought,

Nor shall dull Brit take thy
image to their aid,
When in nocturnal times to
bed they hoard;
So long as men shall thieve,
we wish to see,
Less large excess, and greed
give life to thee.

Hey Rick, I'm out of cash, you got any Monet?

The TV cooking competition 'The Jagged Wok' is entered by a talented council house lad, from Doncaster.

Grabbawoky

'Twas grilli'g, and the spicy toast
Did fire and tremble and degrade:
All flimsy were the hollow globes,
And the toast racks displayed.

'Beware the Jagged Wok my son!
The cloves that bite, the freaks that watch!
Beware the custard bird, and shun
The glutinous butter - scotch!.'

He took his forthright fork in hand:
Long time the toothsome roe he sought-
Ingested he the hung mung bean.
And good lambs fry he bought.

And, there in stylish wrought there stood,
His Asda wok upon the flame
(Came with a lid, as usually would)
He filled it up with game.

Swan too? Gone! Flew! And stew and brew
This portion made was not a snack!
And it is said, he used his head
His own triumphing knack.

And he did gain the Jagged Wok.
Thumbs up! 'Stay calm, Oh steamish boy
Oh fabulous day,' ' O'er moon! Hooray!'
He chuckled in his joy.

Twas brilliant, and the bubbly toasts
Did fire the vict'ry on parade,
All kingsy were the pheromones,
And the home rats outplayed.

10.

(Steiff, Russ and Hermann are all makes of teddy-bears – which have a very close connection with my children's upbringing.)

Bearpurloin

What is this Steiff if dull of hair,
We have no crime for filching bears.

No crime at hand on wide playgrounds
Is where a cry alarming sounds.

Though crime we see when shops we pass,
Where felons seize the Russ break glass.

Sometimes we see in broad daylight
Toys ursine on shelves at height.

And time a turn a backward glance
To watch the pilfering advance.

And time to gain the lost Hermann,
Now filched within a transit van.

A poor life this if no one cares,
We must recoup these stolen bears.

He's upset because he needs surgery to remove his wallet.

The following poem is based on a character who has a slight drug problem.

The Traffords' Ills

I floated vainly with a crowd
That boats on high o'er bales and sills,
When all at once I said out loud
'I must pay those Stafford bills,
Before they take offensive fees,'
muttering and dancing wet striptease.

Innocuous day that started fine
Though crinkles were a silky grey,
I dreamt a never ending line
Along the margin of a tray,
Then Bronta saw I in a trance
Flopping their legs in sprightly dance.

The veins inside were lanced but they
Undid the wanton need in me.
I knew it was not wise to pray
On such a fetid larceny.
I lazed and gazed, a little fraught
And wealth was low and I was caught.

In need when to my pouch I buy
To brighten up my 'pressive mood,
I hear a trenchant inward cry
(Which is not blind decrepitude!)
And then my mind with zany fills
And dances 'midst those ganja pills.

Baggin Court

Once more unto the beach,
dear friends, once more;
And make up the sarnies
from our English bread!
At work there's nothing so becomes us all
As modest humour and keen loyalty:
But when the end of term sounds in our ears,
Then imitate the action of the sprinter;
Stiffen the luggage, summon up the passport,
Disguise fair freckled skin
with mild flavoured lotion.

Then lend the wallet hearty wads
of travellers cheques;
Let it bulge through the lining of the suitcase
Like the pocket parked apple;
Let unbridled joy o'erwhelm the senses
As wonderfully as do the mem'ries
Of years gone by
when beaches were assailed,
Swill'd by th' defiled and waste full ocean.
Now set the sat. nav.
and service the engine whine,
Hold hard the handles
and pile the bulging cases
To their full height!
On, on you merry travellers!
Whose time has come
for exit from employment;
You employees, that like so many others,
Have in these parts s'milar exits sought
And packed their bags for imminent departure.

Prepare to follow your neighbours,
who at the barbecue you saw,
those whom you called friends
and did invite you,
Drink coffee now,
then join the airline flood,
And gridlock the M4.
And you good children,
Whose inflatables were made in Taiwan,
show us here
The texture of your ice cream,
let us swear
That they are worth their licking;
which I doubt not;

For there is none of you so stayed and blind
That hath not seen the sunshine in the skies.
I see you jump like greyhounds with the ticks,
Straining upon the start. The hols are here:
Follow your parents; and upon their commands
Cry "Go for Harrich, Ireland or Salerno!"

*YHA dormitory notice - Beds will be made up, as laid
down by the standing committee.*

The trials of Fashion Slave Kate

Thrice the thin-fed Cath hath stewed,
Spies her lumps, her edge big-lined?
Shaplier thighs in time must find,
Frowned about the cord run grow;
Thin the choisest bent rails throw,
Moan, chat on the gold phone,
Gaze at tights size thirty one?
Sheltered heaven, creeping bot,
Toil now cursed in the balmed plot.

Stunner struggle, toil at stubble;
Lither yearn, and suction double.

Rip the carton, foil and bake;
Dye to suit, by blow of smog,
Cull of plait and pong of dog,
Chavver's talk, at fine perms spring,
Frizzards edge while jowlets swing,
For the calm of direful trouble,
Like gel-Goth's buoyant double.

Stunner struggle, toil at stubble;
Lither yearn, and suction double.

Rail of rags by youth in sulk;
Riches! Come see more-and gulp
Of the severe short pleat scarf;
Boots on leg long rigg'd f'the park;
Slither to a teeming queue;
Pour on coat, it slips on you,
Silver'd are the jewels she clips;
Pose and lark, if ra-ra fits?
Order of girth strangled cape
Quick delivered by a cab,-
Make accrual quick and grab:
And tear to a chider's floor-run
For the indulgencies of lost caution.

Stunner struggle, toil at stubble;
Lither yearn, and suction double.

Fools we hope you understood,
Fashion's charm is skin-deep crud.

The rain it raineth every day
Upon the just and unjust caller,
But mainly on the just, because
The unjust has the just's fedora.

(With apologies to Charles Bowen).

And another example from 'Verse and Worse'

The Village Blacksmith

Under a spreading gooseberry bush the village
burglar lies,
The burglar is a hairy man with whiskers
round his eyes
And the muscles of his brawny arms keep
off the little flies.

He goes on Sunday to the church to hear
the parson shout.
He puts a penny in the plate and takes
a pound note out
And drops a conscience-stricken tear in case
he is found out.

Anon

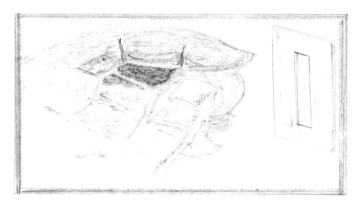

Get Slotted.

Filmstarbilge

I think that I will never see
A poem lovelier than me.

And me whose sultry south
is dressed
Up to my svelte girth's glowing
breasts;

For me who thinks I'm God all day
As fits my steamy charms I pray;

And see me in my underwear
A nest of Cheetos in my care;

See how my bosom's pert and new.
(Do I showcase a low IQ?)

Poems are made by ghouls like thee,
But only wads of cash made me.

*Smirk-voiced, mannered, unctuous gas bag – not unlike
certain radio 3 presenters.*

Tearlingporkies

What a wonderful od'ur* the pig are---
When he grunt he speak almost;
Where he live, his stay…. almost.
He ain't got no wings hardly;
He dont get no mail hardly either.
When he sing, he sing 'bout what he ain't
pot or roast. (Yet)

* Pronounced 'oh – der' with emphasis on 2nd syllable

…and you thought you had a bad night!

Lieder Here

Arnold is fanatical about his garden and is outraged by his neighbour's cat which keeps depositing offensive material in his rose bed and then spending hours basking in the sun on an old cushion within arms reach, on the other side of the hedge. He plans to make a device which will replace the cushion and end his problem.

Cremoggymate

When the thread is drawing
Round the polyester storing,
When the charge is in there
With the three-fuse waiting for me.
Got me no TNT
But I'll see to that,
Yes it won't be pretty
When I kill my neighbour's cat!

Is this the way to arm-a-pillow
Every night I've been hiding in willow,
Really seems I've armed a pillow
And sweet revenge it waits for me.

Blow me away I've armed a pillow,
I've had jeebies, I'm not mellow,
Trying covers on a pillow
I'll go and get the TNT.

Sha la la ia Ia ia ia ia (X 3)
(Loud explosion)
And sweet oblivion's here for me.

There's a church bell ringing,
There's the sound of people singing
Ave Maria.
Means this guy's not going to be there.
I'm beyond the skyway,
Spy an open plain,
And I keep on going,
Wont be back again.

It is not wise to arm a pillow,
I'm a recent departed fellow,
I wish I hadn't armed a pillow,
Should not have used the TNT.

(Holy choir sings) Sha la la ia Ia ia ia ia (X 3)
Repeat and fade.

God may forgive you, but your Mrs wont.

(My son became a white van man.)

I'm still in love with my van

Chorus: You can keep your truck
You can keep your Ford
A Rollers fine
For a toff or a Lord,
But for me it's the way that I am,
'Cause I'm still in love with my van.

With my foot to the floor
Tuned to radio 1
With my arm on the door
With my sun shades on.
You won't catch me in a Merc or a tram,
Cause I'm still in love with my van.

Chorus:

While I look at the view,
Coming up to the ton,
At a hundred and two,
With my hazards on!
It won't annoy me to be caught in a jam,
Cause I'm still in love with my van.

Chorus:

And for hours I sit
Which will give you a clue,
Why my trousers don't fit
'Cause my a**e size grew.
And I will give a lift to my gran
Cause I'm still in love with my van.

Chorus:

(After final chorus)

**It's like riding round in my pram,
That's why I'm still in love with my van.**

Bodger's Lodge Ltd.

(The following poem 'Boatheavian Crapsody' is based on
the following story after a family argument, Mark, a well-
meaning, but incompetent teenager, is at sea in a small
boat to try and catch fish to keep his mother's failing chip
shop business afloat. He is phoning for the lifeboat whilst
the unfamiliar rocking of the boat is having predictable
consequences.......)

Boatheavian Crapsody

Is this the real strife
Is this just fallacy?
Thought in my mind slides
Row, escape from normality.
(Very sea sick)
Thinking of fries
Hook up for the pies and tea.
Oh----poor joy
Because my queasy tum, eas'ly goes,
Middle high, middle low,
Anyway the wind blows
really really matters to me, to me.

Mama, just chilled a van.
'Do your best' is what she said,
Now the trigger fish is dead.
Mama the tide has just begun
And now I've gone and cast my line away.
Mama, ooh,
Always hoped to let you fry.
If I'm not back by train this time tomorrow
Carry on, carry on, as if nothing really matters.

To date my chyme's not come.
My dinner's on my mind
Body's wretching all the time.
Flood by everybody, I'm good to go,
I will leave it all behind and change the tune.

(Boat rocking and wind increase alarmingly)

Mama, ooh (any way my wind blows)
I want you to fry,
I sometimes wish I'd never been aboard at all.

I see a little pirouetto of a prawn
Shovelnose, Shovelnose
you are not from Vendango.
(Holding small fish)

Thorneyhead and whiting
Isnt really brightening me.
(Sacramento) Sacramento!
(Sacramento) Sacramento!
Sacramento Danio!
Mud minnow go!

I'm just a saw boy and somebody loves me.
He's just a saw boy from a raw family
Spare him his life from this monster of sea.

Queasy come, queasy go, It wont let me go,
Fish killer! No, please don't make me throw
(Set him low!) Fish killer!
Please don't make me throw –

(Set him low!) Fish killer!
Please don't make me throw –
(Set him low!) Please don't make me throw –
(Set him low!) Please don't make me throw –

(Never, never, never let me throw) Up!

Oh, Oh, Oh, Oh, Oh, Oh, No.

(Oh Mam I fear,
dihorea's what I fear, let me show

Poseidon has a weevil put aside for me,
for me, for me.

(He becomes delirious – lifeboat on the skyline)

So you think you can clone me
and spit in my fly.
So you think you can glove me
and I'll get to try.
Oh lady, won't do this to me, lady,
Trust oughta get out, Trust oughta
get right outta here.

(Lifeboat rescues him)

(Oh yeah Oh, yeah)

(Mother)
Something really matters
I hope that you can see.
It's you that really matters
(Holding up small fish caught earlier)
But nothing really batters for tea.

(Any way my wind blows)

11.

(Based on the song 'My Way')

Cock-up Cook

And now the end is near
And so I face the final sturgeon
My friend there was that year
I cooked a skate for Richard Burton.

I've made a raspberry fool
And sold them on, on Smallbrook Ringway
And more, much more than this
I worked at Fryways.

Vinaigrettes I've made a few
But then again too few to mention
I sliced what I had to stew
And puréed too, to get attention.

I planned each separate course
Each pukka dish whilst singing 'My way'
And more, much more than this
I worked at Fryways.

Yes there were times I'm sure I knew
When they bit off more than they could chew
But through it all when there was trout
They ate it up and spat it out,
the boss did bawl
Back to the wall!
When I worked at Fryways.

I've peeled, I've chipped and fried,
The dishes were not of my choosing
And now the boss is snide
I find it all rather bruising.

To think I cooked all that
And may I say not in a Thai way
Oh no, not Starbucks me
I worked at Fryways.

For what is a flan what has it got?
If not a crust then we must not
Just add the things it truly needs
And not to mind the way it feels
But the record shows my flans had holes
When I worked at Fryways.

...and he could always cook up a
fresh excuse if it were needed.

(This is based on the song 'Bridge Over Troubled Water.')

Anthem to Doomed Cooking

When you're clearly
Steaming pork.
When meat has filled your pies
I will try them all.
Rinds on the side.
Sometimes it's tough
But keep your cool (don't frown).
Like the fridge by the puddled water
It will lay steam down.
Like the fridge by the puddled water
You may want to drown.

When it's down the spout
When you're in a stew.
When puddings sets so hard
I will laugh with you.
I'll try your tart,
When it's rock hard
And stains are all around.
Like the fridge by the cuisine altar
You may wear a crown.
Like the fridge by the cuisine altar
You will soon turn brown.

*(U tube – Fridge repair man visits kitchen – he leaves –
later cook phones – repair man returns – cook happy fridge
ok – thumbs up.)*

Capon silver grill
Baste and fry.
Your wine was mixed with brine
Now it's in the sky.
See how it binds
With Tate and Lyle
And now quite soon you'll find.
Like a fridge that's a double faulter
You won't have to mind.
Like a fridge that's a double faulter
Sugar's less refined.

Sizzle

Sizzle

Sizzle

Splat!

A middle aged infants teacher surveys her current class.

Pesterday

Pests today, all my students seem
to be at play,
Now I wish that they would
float away,
Oh there will be no rest today.

Luckily, it's not half the hour
it used to be,
But there's a target hanging over me,
End of term is near you see.

Why they are so slow I don't know
(brain cells too few?)
(holds nose)
I sense something strong it must
be on someone's shoe.

(Dreaming)
Saturday, I was shopping
and I'm glad to say,
That I've sorted out my holiday,
Hiking down the Pennine Way.

(Back in classroom)
When will their minds grow,
it's as if they're made of clay.
May be wont be long now
before my hair goes grey.

Cant display, work that is already
done today.
When I sleep tonight I'll lie awake.
That surely was a less hair day.
Mm mm mm mm not ok
Mm mm mm mm pesterday.

(An elderly professor of chemistry sits in his laboratory and as a distraction from some of his murderous thoughts, he is changing labels on jars in an attempt to conceal the amounts of poison he will later steal with the motive of poisoning his wife, Dove, because she bullies and humiliates him in public. He is also mildly infatuated with a good looking laboratory assistant, Meg. Based on Robbie Williams – 'Angels')

Labels

I sit here late
Does a label complicate my life?
And does she know
The places where they go?
Now I'm grey and old,
Cause I haven't been told,
That cessations in my mind unfold,
So when I'm lying in my head,
Thoughts running through to Meg
And I wish that Dove was dead.
I'm moving labels instead.

But through it all she hammers me correction,
And not of love and affection,
Whether I'm bright or strong,
And Dove I'll slaughter, fall,
However it may shake me
I know that she wont break me,
When she comes to maul, she wont placate me.
I'm moving labels instead.

When I'm feeling bleak,
And the stain moves up a one layer sheet
I hook above,
And I know I'll always be vexed with Dove
And now the feeling grows,
She'll wreak flesh from my bones
And when Dove is dead
(shakes head – he clearly does not want to kill her)
I'm moving labels instead.

But through it all she hammers me correction
And not of love and affection
Whether I'm bright or strong
And Dove I'll slaughter, fall,
However it may shake me
I know that she wont break me,
When she comes to maul, she wont placate me.
I'm moving labels instead.

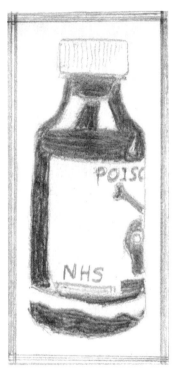

The strictly teetotal old lady died, and in her cupboard
they found dozens of empty cough mixture bottles. The
main content of the mixture was alcohol!

(When I was a Primary school music teacher I sometimes tried my hand at writing words for the children to sing. These words fit to the melody of the song 'Tomorrow belongs to me' from the musical 'Cabaret'. If there are any music teachers out there in need of a new song for a harvest festival then please be my guest, there is no copyright on this page.)

Harvest Song

The apples shine brightly and swing in the breeze,
The corn in the meadow stands tall,
The bramble has covered the hedge with ease,
The harvest delights us all.

The insect that flies for the swallow in flight,
The cone in the forest that falls,
The mushroom that nestles away from the light,
The harvest delights us all.

The trout in the river with silvery gleam,
Vaults high in the waterfall,
The pollen of flowers enfolds the bee,
The harvest delights us all.

The wholesome* prize of allotment and field,
The produce will ripen and store,
To nurture and cherish throughout the year,
The harvest delights us all.

* Please note that on the first line of verse four - the first syllable of 'wholesome' requires two notes

White Richmist

I'm dealing with a site wish-list
Just like the one I think you know,
And the interests risen,
by forecasts driven,
Will raise the overdraft I grow.
I'm dealing with a site wish list,
With ev'ry troll email I write.
May your bills at Christmas be slight
And may all your purchases be light.

(I spend a great deal of time on a volunteer allotment, with the aim of growing fruit and vegetables, some of which goes to the local food-bank and some to the Volunteer Centre who either turn it into jams or chutney or soup. (Based on 'The Sound of Silence'.)

Lum Bard

Hello backache my old friend
I've come to know you as I bend,
Above the soil the Jenny was creeping
And it left its seeds that I was treating
And the feeling that was planted in my spine,
While I recline,
Became the pound of backache.

And at the plot I worked alone,
Finding glass and bits of bone
With no shelter from the cold and damp,
I made the soil into a three foot clamp
When my fingers were stamped by the sting,
of a nettle's leaf,
I grit my teeth
And that was with the backache.

And in the new raised bed I saw
Ten thousand dock plants maybe more
The bed I saw myself it was leaking,
And the answer that I was seeking,
And the restfulness that muscles never got
I'd lost the plot
Which meant a lot of backache.

Fools said I, I did not know
Why comfrey like a true weed grows.
For it causes pain that is profound,
My joints were making a creaking sound,
When the comfrey needed strimming with a knife,
We'll get a life,
Added to the backache.

And Robert wrestled with a spade
Near the heap that he had made,
And Dean he shouted out a loud warning
That the thunder clouds they were forming,
And as Lisa saw the fall of the
water on the tunnel door we all withdraw,
To contemplate the backache.

(Scene from the musical 'Mac-aint-able' by Steepon Songhighs)

Anne a primary school teacher is on an arranged date with Mac an uncouth, loud-mouthed, unintelligent, scaffold erector who hasn't showered. Sally, Anne's friend whose idea this was, said that she'd been told Mac was 'well endowed' and that he drives a sports car. The latter, as Anne knows to her cost is definitely true - he seriously scared her, on their trip to the restaurant and he is now making obscene comments while eating his pork leg noisily.

(Please bear in mind that this poem reflects the subject matter by, at times, using crude language.)

Anned Another Thing

The minute you hawked up a joint,
I could see you were a man of expunction,
A real sick gender,
Flood puking, so reviled.
Nay you wouldn't be likely to know what's
going on in my mind!

So maybe you'll now get the point,
I don't drop my chalk for ev'ry man I see
HEY rig mender,
Wend a little while I flee.

Wouldn't I like to have fun? Fun? RUN!
(Holds nose)
If you'd take a few baths! BATHS!
Your tattoo is a - bad sign
Oh I see that you've – done time!

You idiot you don't get the point,
I can see your fire is now in extinction,
A real dim ember!

*(Mac leaves table to pick up a dropped fork revealing
his builder's bum.)*

Butt crooked, so behind.
Nay you wouldn't be likely to know what's
going on in my mind!
You still have not quite got the point,
I would rather date an ape from Mozambique
HEY Pig blender,
HEY Stick vendor,
HEY Stig minger

END ___ this sick'ning time with me.

Pataquery

Linda was off to
university
with cash to spare.
She thought she could now
afford a car
or a boyfriend.
Her dad's advice was simple.
He said 'Remember,
If
it's got tyres or testicles
It'll give you trouble.'

Lucky Jim (How I envy him)

Jim and I as children played together.
Best of chums for many years were we.
I alas, had no luck, was a Jonah;
Jim my chum was lucky as could be.

CHORUS: Ah! Lucky Jim, how I envy him!
Ah! Lucky Jim, how I envy him!

Years passed by. Still Jim and I were comrades.
He and I both loved the same sweet maid.
She loved Jim and married him one evening.
Jim was lucky. I unlucky stayed.

CHORUS: Ah! Lucky Jim, how I envy him!
Ah! Lucky Jim, how I envy him!

Years rolled on and death took Jim away, boys,
Left his widow and she married me.
Now we're married, oft I think of Jim, boys,
Sleeping in the churchyard by the sea.

CHORUS: Ah! Lucky Jim, how I envy him!
Ah! Lucky Jim, how I envy him!

Charles Horwitz..

Chasedergeld

And did those feet in patient lines,
Wait upon Sainsbury's cash machine:
And was this wholly fanned in wads,
From England's 'gregious
banks obsene!
And did the counter dance supine,
File more upon their mounted tills?
And was John Lewis store
builded here,
To sting with stark gigantic bills?

Bring me my Rover sprayed like gold;
Bring me the cruiser I desire:
Bring me my beer: in h'ppy'our sold!
Bring me my p'wer-driver on hire!
I will not cease from cost-cut flight,
Nor shall I stay my credit hand:
As they have built a new Poundland,
In England's greed infested land.

Another very memorable experience came from listening to the songs of Michael Flanders and Donald Swann. Absolute comic brilliance. I would also recommend the song 'The Oldest Swinger in Town'

Risqué Business

Stereo-trypes

This writer here you'll say he lied
(And later he was vilified)
For telling of a sad event
But to depress was never meant.
He spread the word to all he knew
A story he averred was true
(A sea tale that's in no way dull,)
but probably apocryphal.

The ship it sailed well out of view
Replete with tourists, stores and crew,
But tragedy was yet in store
Ineptitude the Captains flaw,
The mighty vessel struck a reef
And quickly was soon underneath
The waves, and leaving mournful cries
Of those who had, with luck, survived.

They landed on th'uncharted isle
A place that would the mind beguile,
A land perhaps of recent birth
You'll find it not on Google earth.
And gathered there upon the sand
A very cosmop'litan band
Of people who that we could say
Were glad to be alive that day.

There were
Two Italian men and one woman,
Two Greek men and one woman,
Two French men and one woman,
Two German men and one woman,
Two English men and one woman.

The Italians were a touch extreme,
In manner not at all serene,
The males, Benito and Caesar
Began a heated sharp fracas
They really had a lot to gain
O'er who should bed the fair Helene
And she was filled with fear and dread
When Caesar shot Benito dead.

And in the sun the handsome Greeks
Had partied on, all laughs and shrieks,
Cavorting wildly in the sea
(It would have made some cheap TV)
The men had then both disappeared
The woman searched but as she feared,
(You could have felled her with a feather)
She found them bedded well together.

The French were in a blissful state,
Their joie de vivre I can relate
Was fulsome rounded and I found
They made a most arousing sound
For they, Oh Yes, were making hay,
And all at once I have to say
A carry on, a la-di-da
A carefree blissful ménage a trois.

The Germans they were organised
(No 'sturm und drang'! You'd be surprised,)
The Frau she had no lasting doubts
She didn't want two sour Krauts,
For bedroom time filled with delight
She'd framed and mounted in plain sight,
A schedule which we all could tell
Was typed and printed on excel.

(By contrast however.....)

The English folk were looking glum
As hush! Keep schtum! Was rule of thumb,
And they were looking tense and stressed
As if some crime had been confessed.
The silence had an air of dread
For no word had as yet been said,
And then the answer was produced
No one had been introduced.

But me speak first – NO WAY HOSEA!

(This was inspired by the reported incident of a shoplifter who concealed a frozen chicken under his hat while queueing at the checkout the cold caused him to faint.)

Shopped

Dido Andropolis
Lived in Metropolis,
Shoplifted some cheese in her bra.
The curds and the whey
Ran together that day, (which meant)
She was moist with her known Feta.

Pregnant Pause

The midwife strained and slightly fraught
Prepared for the outcome we all sought.
An ectopic pregnancy an early birth
Not a time for levity or mirth
She said:
'The child will soon be here to greet us.'
And thought
'Let's hope the situation does not de-foetus.'

Buy a duffel coat for your one year old and he'll soon be a toggler.

Uswine

The DVD box in my hand shows a shop-front
with an angular sign comprising of three balls.
In the foreground is photomontage
Of two Tamworth Sandyback pigs
with private parts enlarged.
Oh dear,
I appear to have selected a film from the
Pawn'hog'raphy section.

*I remember singing this song at Langdale Junior School,
Clayton, Newcastle Under Lyme in 1961.*

Riding down from Bangor, on an eastbound train,
After weeks of hunting, in the woods of Maine,
Quite extensive whiskers, beard,
mustache as well,
Sat a student fellow, tall and slim and swell.

Empty seat behind him, no one at his side,
Into quiet village, eastern train did glide,
Enter aged couple, take the hindmost seat,
Enter village maiden, beautiful, petite.

Blushingly she faltered, 'Is this seat engaged?'
Sees the aged couple, properly enraged,
Student's quite ecstatic, sees
her ticket through,
Thinks of the long tunnel, thinks
of what he will do.

Pleasantly they chatted, how the cinders fly,
Til the student fellow, gets one in his eye,
Maiden sympathetic, turns herself about,
"May I if you please sir, try to get it out?"

Then the student fellow, feels a gentle touch,
Hears a gentle murmur, 'Does it hurt you much?'
Whiz! Slap! Bang! Into the tunnel quite,
Into glorious darkness, black as Egypt's night.

Out into the daylight glides that eastern train,
Student's hair is ruffled, just the merest grain,
Maiden seen all blushes when then and there
appeared,
A tiny little earring, in that horrid student's beard.

Louis Shreve Osborne

Eurostar enters Mrs Thatcher's back passage!

(My Friday nights go swimmingly.)

Life Savour

A splash of colour
In my blurred vision.
Hoisted above the wet deck,
Sitting serene, seventeen and
unflustered,
Ever watchful for unsurfaced
swimmers.
Long limbed, legs akimbo,
Scarlet shirt and sexy shorts.
Oh my nubile nymphet,
How I've come to deep end on you.

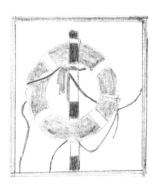

Supplied with or without infilling of cement.

(A Knight and a Reeve meet on a road near the King's castle.)

Gaylord

'Good Sir Knight, how faireth our aged King?
Are we to be blessed with an heir?'

'Alas Reeve, he is still intent
upon bedding local knaves.'

'Then abandon hope as his
life enters its final chapter?'

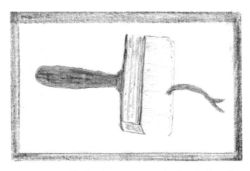

The courtesan's bedroom needed a lick of paint.

'Aye, though I dare say.....
it will run to a good few more pages.'

Wallbanger

When it comes to the matter of sexuality
and the sensuous coating of freshly plastered,
conjoined walls then I tell you size matters.

12.

Oh what a ....

Brief on Counter

And it's home now to Floxbury Mansions
To onions and scallops sautéed,
With some saucy knicks
That're risqué small bits
For she who must be outréd.

Date a Dictionary

Picture it for yourself
there I was sitting
In an up market Lesbian restaurant,
Sorry Lebanese restaurant
Opposite Hedda Précis,
A stunning Lexicographer
Currently re-writing the
OED no less.

I was having a little dalliance,
i.e. having a night away from
my long-time partner Theandre.
It was one of those phrases
you go through when
we'd reached a period,
where I felt the need to dash off
and instigate another introduction.
The contents of my life
having become a little type cast.

Hedda had a degree
(Though she claimed she'd got it,
by plagiarising her fathers
finals paper answers
– a blatant case of parent thesis –
if ever I heard one.)
Hedda was bright alright
But that wasn't what I'd Met her for!
My eyes were drawn to her
Aglobe pepetua split infinitives
that I wished to fontle.
At this point Subjunctivitis
was franklin an ocular possibility.

Then Hedda sneezed,
(she'd obviously caught an inflection),
And this may have been a signal,
(the subtext to all this was probably
what she had been doing
with her mobile phone under the table)
For in walked my lady

Yeah Thea saw us!
And abbreviated our relationship
before a crossword had been said.
'What kind of an idiom do you take me for',
Bawled Thea.
(Scene deleted)
Well that put a full stop to it all.
I was out in the Britannic bold
Definitely comic, sans the humour
And the whale thing makes me [sic]

Is Your
Tahoma in a coma?

Adapted from an article in the Welsh Friendsheep Ewespaper

Billionaire Immorald Chump
forcibly purchased
An area of coastline near Borth,
Including all the larger sand hills,
(Used for stamina building by Olympic trainers)
And in incandeescent haste
had them fenced them off
with barbed wire.
Much to the fierce opposition of the local
population.
Privately it is believed,
through ear witness reports
of fires and strange chantings,
that the land has been given over
to certain groups who revere satanic worship.
Signs attached to the wire
meant to deter athletes and day walkers
say the site has been declared an SSSI
though the rather overblown
graffiti may be more accurate :
Site of sodomite saturnalian insidiousness.
That's the situation,
I can comment no further
Except to remark
That in Borth it would seem
the devil has all the best dunes.

Here's another rhyme from my friend Andy

A man is not old when his
hair turns grey,
A man is not old when his
teeth decay,
But a man is heading for his
last long sleep,
When his mind makes promises
his body can't keep!

Limericks

There was an old man of Khartoum,
Who kept two tame sheep in his room.
With one his intentions
Were as De Sade mentions,
The other was kept as a broom.

God's plan made a hopeful beginning
But man spoiled his chances by sinning.
We must trust that the story
Will end in God's glory,
But at present the other side's winning.

Anon

A spouse-seeking midget called Kate,
Found her beau, at the golf club, green eight.
And aft'r a lark in the park,
She was heard to remark,
'The size of this member's first rate.'

In pursuing a young Prince from Burma,
A gold-digger found him a slow learner,
So she completely undressed
Though he looked unimpressed,
Yet the line of his trousers got firmer.

African Royal Sceptre – no disrespect intended.

My daughter said – 'My colleague asked me to fill a
slot at an innuendo conference.'
(There's no answer to that.)

(The following poem just had to be included- it has
been described as 'doggerel' but hook airs.)

Ode To Those Four-Letter Words

Banish the use of those four-letter words
Whose meanings are never obscure.
The Angles and Saxons, those bawdy old birds,
Were vulgar, obscene and impure.
But cherish the use of the weak-kneed phrase
That never quite says what you mean;
For better you stick to your hypocrite ways
Than be vulgar, or coarse, or obscene.

When *Nature is calling,* plain-speaking is out,
When ladies, God bless 'em, are milling about,
You *make water*, *wee-wee*, or *empty the glass*;
You can *powder your nose*, '*Excuse me*' may pass;
Shake the dew off the lily, see a man 'bout a dog;
Or when everyone's soused, it's *condensing the fog*,
But be pleased to consider and remember just this -
That only in Shakespeare do characters ****!

You may speak of *a movement*, or *sit on a seat*,
Have a passage, or *stool*, or simply *excrete*;
Then groan in pure joy in that smelly old shack.
You can go l*ay a cable*, or do *number two*,
Or *sit on the toidy* and *make a do-do*,
Or say to the others, 'I'm going out back',
But ladies and men who are socially fit
Under no provocation will go take a ****!

When your dinners are hearty with onions and beans,
With garlic and claret and bacon and greens;
Your bowels get so busy distilling a gas
That Nature insists you permit it to pass.
You are very polite and you try to *exhale*
Without noise or odour – you frequently fail –
Expecting a zephyr, you carefully start,
But even a deaf one would call it a ****!

A woman has *bosoms,* a *bust* or a *breast*.
Those *lily-white swellings* that bulge 'neath her vest;,
They are *towers of ivory*, *sheaves of new wheat*;
In a moment of passion, *ripe apples* to eat.
You may speak of her nipples as *small rings of fire*
With hardly a question of raising her ire;
But by Rabelais' beard, she'll throw fifteen fits
If you speak of them roundly as good honest ****.

Two verses omitted try www.

Banish the use of those four-letter words
Whose meanings are never obscure.
The Angles and Saxons, those bawdy old birds,
Were vulgar, obscene and impure.
But cherish the use of the weak-kneed phrase
That never quite says what you mean;
For better you stick to your hypocrite ways
Than be vulgar, or coarse, or obscene.

'I'm glad pigs can't fly' said young Sellars,
(He was one of them worrying fellas)
'If pigs could fly
Then they'd poo in the sky,
And we'd all have to carry umbrellas.'

From page _2_
Daredaygo fortylorisinaro
(Dare day go forty lorries in a row)
Demarntloris demartrux
(Dem arn't lorries demare trucks)
Fullacowsan ensandux
(Full of cows and hens and ducks.)

Possible answers to captions

1. ....larking around.
2. ....to take a leek.
3. King of Spades
4. ....the hottest thing in town.
5. I phone you.
6. ....a film on the road.
7. It's Tiger Woods
8. Newcastle under Slime
9. Bear with me.
10. ....Fryway's flyaways.
11. ....sauce.

And Shakespeare should have the last word,
When all's said and Donne.

Index of first lines

A bishop who was ready,
About fifty years ago my father was entrusted
A Delboy twitcher, Albert Ross,
A friend of mine had ghostly experience.
After having a minor tiff with his partner, Mike
A heinous sex tourist named Horrocks
A lady from a wealthy family,
A mad lad who came from Stotfold,
A man is not old when his hair turns grey
An accident happened to my sister Dot,
An accident happened to my brother Jim
An aged lady Margaret Brown,
And now the end is near
And the Lord said unto Moses,
And forgive Maxis Crewe
And have you heard about the Italian lady's
dilapidated Vauxhall
And it's home now to Froxbury Mansions
And then there's old Pap
An indian from the old wild west
A policeman pulls over a speeding car,
A rare old bird is the pelican;
As I was going up a stair,
A splash of colour
A spouse-seeking midget called Kate,

Banish the use of those four-letter words
Before we were married
Billionaire Immorald Chump

Beneath this smooth stone,
Bud beer's at 'The Spring'

Cleopatra believed that the Nile
Commonly heard in England
Crossing merry England was a bishop who was ready

Daredaygo fortylorisinaro
Der spring is sprung
Dido Andropolis Lived in Metropolis,
Doctor Bell a cell did cage,
Doctor Bell fell down a well,
Doctor Blue as wise men do

Every morning at seven o'clock
Ewan kissed me by the spring
Excuse my sodding French

Forgive Balid Cruz

God 's plan made a hopeful beginning
Good King Wenceslas looked out
"Good Sir Knight, how faireth our aged King?"

Happy worm day to you,
Hark, the herald angels sing,
Have you heard the one about the drug pusher
He came from a family of talented acrobats
He grabbed me round my slender neck
He – I drink in your pink chin.
Hello backache my old friend
Here lies Jean Wright,

Here lies John Bunn
Here lies my wife
How useful it would be if How useful it would be if

I am described by all my friends
I am pondering whether to write a singing drama
I'd have liked to been a fly on the wall,
I drink in your pink chin.
I eat m peas with honey
I floated vainly with a crowd
I have a favourite brother
I'm dealing with a site wish-list
I must go down for the cheese again,
In a sea of guilt he floundered
In pursuing a young Prince from Burma,
I sit here late
I think therefore I am.
Is this the real strife
It happened on a Polynesian isle,
I sat next to the duchess at tea;
I view he sliced beetroot that stains
I was in my office
I wish I had not bought a ticket
I wish I was a little grub
I work at Mactavishes

Jim and I as children played together.
Jingle bells, Batman yells,

Last night I killed my cheating wife,
Let me not to marriage of two dykes

My deft Macaw likes aspirins
My father threw me in,

Oh give me a phone,
Once more unto the beach,
One fine day in the middle of the night,
Our Nirvana

Pests today, all my students seem to be at play
Picture it for yourself

'Quarkdom of Skin-Freaks'

Robin, Will and Johners were members of the Hoody
family.

Said Miss Farrow, on one of her larks:
Salutation to the nice lady on the bacon machine in
Sainsbury's
See the happy moron,
Shall I compare thee to a weathered rake?
She stood on the bridge at midnight
Sir, I admit your general rule,

The apples shine brightly and swing in the breeze,
The boy stood on the burning deck,
The chief defect of Zaida Zing
The consummate works of Jane Austin
The DVD box in my hand shows a shop-front
The following conversation took place on a trip
to the dentist.
'The Greek Olympiad begat

The Hippo is a pretty bird
The Lord is my iPhone;
The midwife strained and slightly fraught
The minute you hawked up a joint,
The property was advertised
The spouse-seeking midget called Kate,
The writings of Joseph Von Elevent
This writer here you'll say he lied
There are several reasons for drinking,
There was an old fellow from Lympne
There was an old lady of Ryde
There was an old man from Calcutta
There was an old man from Darjeeling,
There was an old man of Khartoum,
There was an old man of Nantucket
There was a young girl in the choir
There was a young lady from Gage
There was a young lady from Leeds,
There was a young lady named Bright
There was a young lady of Riga,
There was a young lad of St Just
There was a young lady of Tottenham,
They say that when you're in a garden,
This bloody town's a bloody cuss
This writer here you'll say he lied
Thrice the thin-fed Cath hath stewed
'Tis dogs delight to bark and bite
'Twas an evening in September
'Twas an evening in November,
'Twas grilli'g, and the spicy toast
Twas in the month of Liverpool,

162

Under a spreading gooseberry bush the village
burglar lies,

Vespula Engrossopola,

Wandering through an estate
We three kings of Leicester square
What is this Steiff if dull of hair,
When it comes to the matter of sexuality
When I was on line
When the thread is drawing
When you're clearly steaming pork,
While shepherds washed their socks by night
Whilst slimming a young girl – Evette
Whose woods are these I think I know
With life it's hard to get to grips
Without a shower,

Yankee Doodle went to town
You can keep your truck,
You'll never wake a Cheatah Cake
You may have met them

Acknowledgements

Writing poetry for me has always been an expression of happiness at the time of writing therefore, I would like to thank my mother Jessie, my good lady Chris, my children Mike and Steph and my brother Ian. I would also lke to thank my friend Andy Crow.

Other than family and friends my everlasting gratitude goes to the BBC and the array of fantastic humour particularly on radio over the last fifty years.

Thank you for reading this book. If you would like to see any more of my poetry or if you would interested in very rude limericks and jokes then please contact me at a.joynson@tiscali.co.uk

Lightning Source UK Ltd.
Milton Keynes UK
UKOW07f0522100915

258408UK00011B/62/P